result of the use of the information contained within this book, including but not limited too. – omissions, errors, and inaccuracies. Please note most of this publication is based on personal experience and secondary evidence. Use this information at your own expense, there is no guarantee for financial success.

21 DAYS TO A MORE
POSITIVE ME

Work in Progress

BRIDGET MYERS GUNSBY

Dedicated to ~ *my parents, Delores*

and Stanley Myers, who instilled in me the

values that enabled me to endure many

challenging times. I love you both dearly.

Table of Contents

Day Ten

Day Eleven

Day Twelve

Day Thirteen

Day Fourteen

Day Fifteen

Day Sixteen

Day Seventeen

Day Eighteen

Day Nineteen

Day Twenty

Day Twenty-One

Introduction

Begin and end every day with a positive thought.

Often, I long for becoming a new-to-be version of myself. Life can be confusing and it can be a challenge to figure where to begin. I realize it's challenging to change how I am and who I am, even when I know that change is necessary. To be honest, just the thought of change can be downright intimidating. The real question is, what do I change within me? Or do I want to simply talk about wanting change? When I look around, I see people making positive changes and positive adjustments to their lives daily. Such as writers, authors, artists, musicians, community leaders, just to name a few. And even some people I know personally that I feel is on the same playing field as I am, are now living their dream, living their truth and purpose.

Then, the daunting question appears in my head –**Why not me**?

That one question is the wake-up call I desperately needed because the truth of the matter is, I'm not living my true life because I haven't yet made a commitment of putting in the work. Constantly making excuses of why I have not. You know the ones I am talking about—I'm too busy, I'm too tired, I have the kids, I have no help, I would do it if I could or if I had the time… News flash to self, the world is currently set up for the ordinary. Go to school, get a degree, work in that field, or graduate from high school and enter the workforce. Depending on my career choice and how hard I work, I am may be OK financially. However, is that really my passion? Is that really my truth? If I can work hard for this company and help the owner or founder of it stay successful, then why can't I do the same for myself?

I can. I just have to want it badly enough. How badly do I want it? I want it so badly that I lose my breath when thinking about it. I want it so badly that I feel I will die if I don't achieve it. Starting today, I will rid myself of excuses and the words I can't. Today, I come to the realization of there's no such things as impossible instead it's **I'M Possible**. I will make a commitment, I will make a plan and I will work my plan until completion... And each day, while doing so, I will continue to work on me, on becoming the best version of myself. Beginning now! Why now? It's imperative that I begin NOW in order to obtain immediate action. The first step to change is becoming open and available for the change to happen.

Day One

" I shouldn't want to be better than anyone else, I should want to be better than I ever thought I could."- Anonymous.

Welcome to day ONE. I am already one step closer to really staying motivated and becoming the best *ME*. Today is the beginning of the new and improved me, the new and improved you, the new and improved us. Moving forward, I will make a conscious effort on the things that bring me joy. I can acknowledge the fact that, I am a gift to the world and I will strive to make improvements in all areas of my life. I am in control of my own happiness and my actions. The phrase I will carry with me from today forth is-

"How do I want to be remembered when I die, ordinary or extraordinary"?

Knowing that death is inevitable and often untimely, makes me want even more to begin my journey today! I have that irrational phobia for death and dying, the moment I learn to let go of the control it has over me is the moment I can finally pursue what I have been dreaming of doing. I am only *me* once. Shouldn't I try and make the best of it? Don't I want to be able to tell my children, grandchildren, and family that they no longer have to worry? I am the only thing keeping me from reaching as high as possible. Here are a few things to do today to keep me focused and motivated.

1. **Take a big breath and exhale.** Think about breathing in, my lungs filling up with air. Now I hold my breath until I reach the end of this sentence and let out slowly. I just meditated. If I ever feel that I am about to fall out of motivation or feel that I don't want to go on. Do this.

2. **Think of my future.** Let's pretend

winning a race is my main goal of this book. I imagine I am at the finish line grabbing hold that successful bottle of water and envisioning the cheering of my family and friends. Now, if my goal is to own a business, I imagine I am sitting in my successful shop with happy customers. The saying, "If you believe it, you can achieve it" is really true. That is what will drive my motivation and make me stronger.

3. **I know I might fail.** I know that once in a while, I may hit failure, we all may. The best thing to remember is that when that happens, it means I have one less failure to worry about. Soon, I will see it and I will hit it big time. I will not give up after the first negative thought that crosses my mind.

In closing, I will remind myself that I have dreams of becoming someone different than who I am today. The thing that most people don't realize, something that I need to realize as well, is that the only thing keeping me from reaching the highest goal is me. Once I can tell my self-conscious mind to just give it a try, I will really see a change in not just how I look at myself, but how I look at my life.

So, get ready world! Here I come!

Day Two

I will be a better person today than I was yesterday...

*"It's not how good I am. It's how good I **want** to be."*- Paul Arden

It's easy to find flaws in others, I just need to remember that I too have flaws. Today, I will take a long, deep look into a physical mirror as well as an internal mirror. I will write down all the flaws that I would like to change and I will embrace all the flaws I choose to keep. I will also write what adjustments I will put in place in order for the change to happen. Today, I will not focus on what I don't like about a person. Instead, I will solely focus on the things I do like about them, such as their kindness, their smile or even their fashion sense. I realize if I turn my negative radar off, I'm likely to find a positive in all situations. No matter what negative situation that I come across today, I will not give it any energy. I am aware that I am in complete control of me and I am giving and receiving Good Vibes Only.

My mind is my power, if I can convince my mind of something, it will be true. I have to remember that and hopefully motivate my peers and coworkers to think positively too. This will not only help their life, but will improve the work environment and progress. I want to be all that I can be and the first step is recognizing the negative. I need to stop them in their tracks, I will train myself to catch negative thoughts that run through my head, and I will think of how I would feel if someone said that to me. Becoming aware of my own thoughts can really help me gain more self-understanding and empathy. An activity I can try to improve this process-

A Couple of Compliments- I will find someone I know and someone I don't. I will do this once a week, and then eventually every day. Compliments can make the world go around. I know how much I love receiving compliments, and if I can give that same feeling to someone else for free I will, in turn, feel it too. Positivity can be all around us as long as we allow it.

The best thing I can do for myself today is to let others into my new world of being positive and motivating. I deserve this, and so do others.

If I can change the environment around me for the better, I know it will only help me stay motivated in my course to success.

Day Three

Dear Me,

I Dare Myself.

"I will take risks: If I win, I'll be happy. If I lose, I'll be wise." ~ Unknown

I look into the mirror, and what do I see? I take a long, deep stare and love every imperfection I see. From that pimple on my face to the slight gap in my teeth; I dare myself, I dare myself. I say out loud, "today is a day of possibilities". When I have a positive attitude and approach to life, all things are possible. I will repeat the phrase again and again until a smile emerges upon my face, and I feel it in my soul, I dare myself. Even if I don't believe it, I make believe: today is a day for the happiness created within me, **I dare myself**.

I imagine today with no worries of anyone's expectations because the life I am living is mine. While on the bus, driving or walking, I will sing my favorite song and do a little dance with it if I like. I dare myself. I will take a minute to slow things down and notice the beauty and creativity of my scenery. I will see how the clouds paint a perfect picture in the sky. I will breathe in the smell of my city, then release.

I will fill my space with positive energy all day. I will give a warm and friendly smile to every person I greet. When someone says a negative remark, I will say something positive, I dare myself. Today, I give my fear and anxiety the back seat because at this moment they don't exist. I say what I mean and mean what I say (*in an appropriate tone of course*). I become aware of how I feel right now at this moment. If I like it, I will do it again tomorrow, I dare myself. I dare myself to live out loud; I dare myself to be myself.

Daily Dare:

1. I will take a pencil and a paper and write down five things I want to

change about my lifestyle, TV time, unemployment, relationships, whatever I want to be better.

2. Now, I will choose one of those things and write five ways it can be possible. For example, I will find a good book to read when I find yourself wanting to watch TV, or set a timer.

3. I will take one day and practice those five things as best as I can. I will see if they work. If not, that is no problem. It only means I found one way that it doesn't work. Now, I have narrowed down the search to finding the answer. I will never give up.

Day Four

Some will say the glass is half full, some will say it's half empty. I say the glass is filled with unlimited opportunities.

"See the glass half full, and fill it the rest of the way." ~Anonymous

The question isn't rather the content in the glass is an equal or a fair amount. Life is not equal or fair. The real question is what am I going to do with what I have? How strong is my faith? Will I stay on the boat or am I going to walk on the water? I believe in my heart that the possibilities of what I can do are unlimited.

I can either find the negatives and emptiness in my life and ignore them, or I can fill them. I have the power to put whatever I want in my glass. Whether it be wealth, beauty, life, or occupation. I am the filler of my cup. It is me who decides what goes in my cup. What flavors I add and what I keep out. My life is in my control, and as long as I am ready to embrace the unknown I can do anything. The glass never has to *stay* half empty, if I find something to fill it. It can be possible. Life is an ever-flowing stream of knowledge and possibilities, I need to take advantage of that and fill myself with as much as I can.

Day Five

I will take a minute to think the situation through and make the moves that are best for me.

"Ten years from now, I will make sure I can say I chose my life, and I didn't settle for it."- Unknown

I often react to my feelings and emotions. Sometimes giving up sounds so much easier than continuing. I say things when I'm angry that I tend to regret later and make mistakes that I thought I would never make. I realize that chaos has been embedded in me through my DNA. Therefore, it is natural for me to react to circumstances instead of responding to them. As the human being, I am; I am an emotional creature and sometimes let my emotion, aka my passion get the best of me. But not today. Not from this point forward, and I am now fully alert and aware of that. Today I will think rationally and logically. Instead of reacting to a situation, I choose to respond to it. For some, life is difficult and for others, life is not so bad. It has been my experience that life is actually pretty simple. It really comes down to the decisions I make. Either I go to school or not. Either I look for a job or not. Either I become an entrepreneur or not. Either I'm kind to others or not. Life is simply reacting to the decisions that I make.

I choose me. I choose my path and how I want to walk it. If I want to take the wheel and drive myself, or if I will let others drive it for me. So many decisions in my life have been because I was worried what "they" might think. Who cares. I need to choose for me. I am a strong independent person and the only one who can choose the path I take. If I don't want to eat something spicy, I don't eat something spicy. Life choices should be that simple for me to make too and starting today. If I want to do something, I am going to do it.

Day Six

"Fear is the Brain's way of saying that there is something important I need to overcome" – Rachel Huber

I will always say this. I am not afraid of failure. Failure only means I am learning. Failure is the next step to success.

I can do anything I put my mind to, even if I am absolutely terrified. The dream that I have been dreaming about, the project I have been putting off, it can all be done if I choose to do it. That idea that I have been talking about, thinking about, daydreaming about, but have not pursued; for reasons such as... "It's just a thought, but if it **could** happen it would be such a beautiful thing". Or reasons like... "I don't have enough time; there are not enough hours in the day. It doesn't fit my schedule, but if I did have the time it **could** be such a wonderful thing".

However, the biggest reason of all is that I might fail. My fear of failure is so great that I do not believe I could really be successful at whatever I choose to do. That thought ends today. Too many people find that their lives are halted and put on the side because they are afraid to take the leap. I am not afraid.

Today I know that fear does not exist. I will no longer allow fear and excuses to stop me from ever attempting to do what I feel is impossible because I'M possible! I will do it! Yes, I can do it. Contrary to some beliefs, Winners are not winners because they were born that way. Winners are winners simply because they never gave up.

The more I fail, the harder I will succeed, and I am not afraid.

Day Seven

Today I will focus on my breath. I will not breathe shallow breaths, I will breathe and practice diaphragmatic breathing.

"Breathing deeply and releasing fear will help me get to where I want to be." ~Iyanla Vanzant

What happens when I breathe, I feel my lungs fill in and out with air and I can listen to my heartbeat steady. I will focus on my breath and doing it will keep me happier, calmed down, and relaxed. No matter what curve balls this day may have in store for me; I choose to relax and be free from stress. Since diaphragmatic breathing acts as a form of stress relief, I will be mindful and incorporate it into my daily life. As I focus on my breathing today, I will have more energy because I am not stressing. I know that this will play a key part in helping me become a healthier and happier me.

Daily Meditation:

1. I will find a comfortable place to relax.
2. I will close my eyes and count to ten.
3. I will take a deep breath, and think about what the air looks like flowing into my lungs.
4. I will breathe out and imagine the air flying into the air.
5. I will do this five times.
6. I will conquer the day.

If I can take a two-minute pause in my day to meditate and relax, I can let my brain catch up to my ideas and my passions. I will wake up my motivation and feel the success flow through me. I am the master of my day and the controller of my breath.

Today I will breathe. Tomorrow I will succeed.

Day Eight

On this day, I will remove the word "can't" from my vocabulary.

"You want me to do something, tell me I can't do it." Maya Angelou

Whenever someone tells me I can't do something, the first thing I imagine is being able to say "YES I CAN." So what is stopping me? The word "can't" no longer exists in my world, because I don't *want* it, too. As a child, everyone told me I could do anything I want to do if I put my mind to it. As a child, I was told a lot of things by my parents and teachers, however, at the time I unknowingly made the decision to believe the negative. The first time I was ever told: "You can't do that." I began holding myself back.

In all honesty, at the time the negative felt more real to me. I remember watching the Oprah Winfrey show and stating I want to be a successful Philanthropist like Oprah where I could intrigue people with my words and give away cars and such from the kindness of my heart and people would reply "you could never be Oprah" I remember having thoughts of being as brilliant and wealthy as Bill Gates and Paul Allen and as well as sharing the thoughts with my peers and they would tell me "I'm insane, I can't do it. Now, as I have experienced life and I know different. What makes Oprah, Bill or Paul any different from me? The only real difference that matters is they didn't allow the word "can't" to control their lives but I did.

However, today is a new day and "can't" is dead to me. I am all that I choose to be and I can be whatever I like. I will reach for the stars and believe there is no limit to what I can accomplish.

I Can't Exercise: Take 3 simple things I "can't" do: (rollerblade, ski, sing karaoke, jump-rope.)

Now go do one or all of those things. Just *try* them. I will see that it is not that I *can't* do it. It is that I *won't* do it. Once I can learn how to battle the simple things I *can't* do, I will be able to gain courage and conquer the things everyone else thinks I *can't* do. I will prove to them that I CAN.

Day Nine

Today, I will rejoice in the beauty of the day.

"Every morning starts a new page in my story, I will make it a great one today."
~Doe Zantamana

Every day, I have the chance to make something happen, I have the chance to improve what I was yesterday. I have the chance to make someone smile, make someone laugh, and make someone feel great about themselves. So, I should do the same thing to me. I should be able to take a day like today and make it mine. I will thank my creator and enjoy the beauty of life that He has given me. I will indeed take time to smell the roses and to admire the beautiful artistry of the world such as the trees, the birds, the buildings, the grass, the woods the land, the clouds, the moon, the stars, the animals and the humans indeed how unique we are. I know that the production of creating something as magnificent as the moon, stars and the 1st humans are completely out of my control and there's, without a doubt, a creator of the world. And for that, I will show gratitude and appreciation just to be a part of this beautiful art we call life.

Have a "New" Day Exercise

Today I will try something new. Try to make sure every day from now on is filled with something new, whether it is as small as a new flavor of pie, or a new exercise routine. I am in control of me, and who knows what opportunities may await for me just because I did it.
- I will eat something new
- I will listen to something new
- I will go somewhere new
- I will talk to someone new
- I will read/watch something new
- I will smell something new
- I will wear something new

Day Ten

Letting go.

"Forgive and Forget. It may not change the past, but it may at least give the future a chance."- Anonymous

This world I live in is so filled with regret, grudges, and bitterness. I have the opportunity to release myself of that negative weight on my shoulders. Now in this century, nothing is forgotten. People film and take photos, people text and post online. Maybe I have made a mistake in the past, maybe someone I know was the mistake. I need to remember that the past is the past, there is nothing I can do about it now, and that is ok. Because whatever happened, no matter how horrible it may have been, has shaped me here today. Today I am the best me I will ever be, and I need to let myself continue to grow.

People often hold on to what they feel is right. Even if they are dead wrong, my heart might want to stay angry, but my mind knows it's not right. Today I choose to forgive if they are not sorry for their actions- I will forgive them. Not for them, but for me- --Holding onto anger is like carrying a 50lb weight on my shoulders. Carrying weight on my shoulders makes it hard for me to move and be functional. Therefore, I will let it go.

Tips for letting it go myself

Say a Prayer- If I am able to pray and let someone else know what I want to do, it can help me feel less pressure.

I will find the lesson- Everything has a lesson learned. If I can take the pain and the anger and turn it into a learning experience, I will be able to move myself off the blocked path.

Get revenge in success- I will prove to myself that what happened does not define me. I will prove to myself and to others that I am able to continue no matter what may come my way. I am the driver of my own life, and if I choose to let something go, I will.

Day Eleven

Today I will remember.

"Focus on the good habits you want to have, not the bad habit you don't want to have. Overcome the bad with the good." ~ Joyce Meyer.

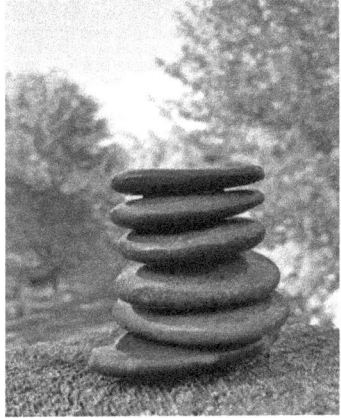

Today marks the halfway point of breaking old habits and becoming a better version of myself. I will also take this time to ponder and focus on how I feel today versus how I felt 10 days ago. Am I happier, calmer, nicer, do I feel the shift?

I will sit in silence for at least 10 minutes today as I reflect over the past 10 days. One minute for each lesson learned. I will also think of how I feel at this very moment. Have I accomplished the goal I set for myself, if not what will it feel like once I accomplish the goals? Today, I will sit and breathe and allow only happy thoughts while paying attention to how I feel at this very moment. And at any time throughout the day when I feel frustrated or flustered, I will go back to my happy thoughts.

I will remember the reason why I am here today, the reason why I wanted to be here in the first place. I am here because I'M POSSIBLE. I am here because I CAN DO IT! I know that because I have made it this far, I know I will not give up. The hardest part is starting out, and I am already halfway through. I am more than what I was yesterday and a better person than I was 10 days ago. I have tried something new, forgiven and let go, learned the importance of patience, understood my own strengths, and helped overcome my fear of failure. I am already well on my way to showing myself and all those around me that I am the BEST that I can be.

Day Twelve

Today I will become a better friend.

"Walking with a friend in the dark is better than walking alone in the light." ~Helen Keller

Life gets overwhelming. That is something I have now come to terms with. It is common that when life gets in the way, we sometimes neglect our friends. Sometimes my work life and family life take all my time and energy. And when I do speak with my pal without thought I make most of our conversations about me and usually focus on my issue at hand. I love my friends and actually depend on their support more than I depend on the support of my significant other. The one thing I should always remember that a friend will always be there. I need to remember the importance of that. My friend is not like family, they were not automatically put into my life, they *chose* it. They *chose* to be a part of my life and I chose them as well. I need to focus on building my outside support. Reconnect with the friends that might be lost, or talk with the friends that are just waiting to hear from me. When life gets in the way, it is the perfect time to find friends because that is when I will need them most. We all have our own interpretation of what "busy" is. And when I feel overwhelmed, I know I can still turn to my friends to help me through this.

Activity: The person you thought of when reading this section, send them a quick message or call them. Just say "Hello" and ask them how they are doing. You thought of them for a reason. Now go.

Day Thirteen

Today I will expect the unexpected

"It's the things you least expect, that hit you the hardest"- Author Unknown

Peace, be still. There are some things that are out of my control such as death and unexpected circumstances, whether they are financial pin-ups or emotional downfalls. I know, they will eventually happen to be. They will try to bring me down and make me weak. This is a mind trick. My mind is

worried and scared about how far I have come, it has never felt this free before. It likes control and when mistakes or unexpected things happen, it tries to comfort me by hiding how I feel and think. However, I need to remember that most things in life I *do* have the power to control, such as a sound mind. I have complete control over my thoughts. Believe it or not, I also have control over my peace and joy. Just because something happens around me, it does not mean it will change my spirit. I am the only one who can do that. No matter what is going on in the world around me, I will stand firm in my decision to hold onto peace and joy no matter what. I will not allow anyone to mess with it, I won't allow anyone to steal it. It belongs to me because I deserve it.

Our minds want answers, the answers I will give will be uplifting and peaceful. I will not let the negative creep into my mind again, I have come so far.

Day Fourteen

Today I will be socially present.

"The present moment is the only moment available to us, and it is the door to all moments"- Thich Nhat Hanh

On the surface, I appear to be very outgoing. No one knows that I'm socially awkward on the inside. Regularly, I will make an effort to blend into the crowd with the hopes that no one outside my peers will talk to me. Though throughout this process, I need to keep one thing in mind. I am only here once. I am only in this moment once. As I grow more confident and upbeat day by day. Just being in the room is no longer good enough. I will always make myself "present" with my smile, grace, helpfulness, and wit. Because the worst thing I can ever be is forgettable. Each moment that passes is another moment I cannot get back. I do not want to sit down in a rocking chair, old and helpless wishing I would have done this or that. So, I will do it. I will do what I have to and make sure that I am making the best of each moment. By being quiet and letting the thought of "what could happen" or "what they might think" I am only hurting myself. Today I take a stand if there is a question I want to ask, if there is someone I want to talk to. I will do it. I won't rely on tomorrow to give me my answers. I will step out of the door and find them myself.

Activity: In a conversation or a moment where I often feel like hiding in the back. I will try to ask a question that I don't know the answer to. No matter how silly, or foolish it might be. The biggest part of it is that I am putting my own knowledge in front of what another person's thoughts might be. That is progress.

Day Fifteen

I will take control of the world by following my goals of compassion.

"Goals allow me to control the direction of change in my favor."- Brian Tracy

The world is truly lacking compassion. I have seen the hate in the world and known that people are constantly feeding and profiting from that. When people profit from hate, it grows until it is uncontrollable. This is OUR world, that WE live in, that makes US responsible for it. I need to show which side of compassion I am on, I need to do my part in protecting and loving those who need it most. I will give my part of volunteering, helping, and catering. Even if I think I am in the worst possible position in life. I need to remember that no matter how bad things get for me, there will always be someone in worse shape. That is what hurts my heart.

People who cannot control their own situation need someone who can to help them. We all must do our part. To help make the world a better place be mindful to have love and compassion for all. I will start by being more mindful of my words, making sure I think before I say things about someone else. I will concentrate on the powers I *do* have and give those when I can. Compassion is lacking in this world, and it is up to me to start the change. I will be that person.

Activity- A minute for a minute- When I find myself thinking negatively, or thinking that I have it bad, once I realize the negative thinking I will look at the clock. If I found I was thinking negative for 5 minutes, 10 minutes, etc. I will add it up at the end of the week. That will be the amount of time I need to spend volunteering my time somewhere. Doesn't matter where, Humane society, donating online, or even just sending a Get well soon to an anonymous person in the hospital. Do something to show love, start the ripple effect.

Day Sixteen

Today I will block out distractions. All of them!

"You can't do big things if you are distracted by small things."- Author Unknown

I know that in my life there will be personal roadblocks I have to overcome, though I need to know when I am making the blocks bigger than they truly need to be. When my mind gets into panic mode I turn into a monster of worry and regret. Distractions are everywhere and have been placed in my life to divert attention away from my goal. The phone, television, friends, and family can all be a form of distraction. Though these are all small things keeping me from reaching my highest potential. I am the one who gets distracted because I control my mindset. Once I have set a goal for myself, I am only hurting my chances if I allow distractions. I can't let anything or anyone stand in the way of me trying to achieve it. Family and friends can be great distractions, or they can be great resources. I need to figure out how to focus my attention on the better parts. If I am constantly stopping over one small thing, or worried about something that does not even have to do with my goal, I am hurting my chances. I am incredibly powerful. My heart is full of desires and dreams, I need to know my demands and how to put them into action.

Activity: 90-minutes. Researchers say the human brain can stay focused for 90-minutes before needing a break. After that, the brain is practically running on fumes. I will take 90-minutes at a time to work with intense purpose. After the time is up, I will reward myself with a well deserved brain break. I may have a cup of coffee and chat for a few with a co-worker or go outside just to have a change of scenery. I will keep a coloring book near and color; Or paper and pens to doodle. I will allow myself time to relax and refocus my mind.

Day Seventeen

I will surround myself with greatness.

" I will surround myself with the people who are only going to lift me higher." - Oprah Winfrey

If I know a person is veering to the left and every time I'm with them I find myself veering to the left as well, I must then recognize this person or people as a form of distraction in my life. I can no longer allow distractions to stand in the way of me accomplishing that I have set for myself. Instead, I will surround myself with greatness. People who think big, dream big and aim high. The feeling of empowerment and greatness is contagious.   I know I will become great, it's inevitable.

Friends and family are there to build me up. I will no longer be embarrassed about my dreams. I will not constantly explain my dreams to anyone. I have the power to be as successful and happy as I choose to be. I will claim my dreams as my own and I will stand firm in my beliefs.

Day Eighteen

I Will Be Honest and Direct.

" I will say what I mean, and mean what I say" -Cheshire cat

I sometimes have a habit of telling people what they want to hear, instead of telling them the truth. When it comes to their wellbeing, I should know that I can tell them

how I really feel. Though I need to remember not to bring them down. If they are passionate and excited about their dream, I need to support them if they want to know my personal opinion on something negative in their life. I need to tell them, exactly how I feel. In becoming a better version of myself, I must practice being open and honest. I will articulate my thoughts, feelings, and ideas in an open and honest manner. In a calm, non-judgmental, non- confrontational tone, I will convey my thoughts as clearly as possible. There's a quote that I read once as listed above, but I am going to add the last part that says " I will say what I mean, and mean what I say, however, I will never say it means". I will commit this phrase to memory and make it a part of my daily habit.

Something I also learned, was normally the harder it is to be said, the *stronger* the reason that it needs to be told. I don't like upsetting my family and friends, but I know if I was in the opposite situation, I would want them to tell me if something was holding me back. If they do not want to listen, then there is nothing more I can do. I need to know that I tried, and in the end, they are the only ones who can truly make the change. I am honest, I am the support, and I will always be there.

Day Nineteen

I Will Be Polite to All.

"Being polite and grateful will make people more inclined to help me. If people are willing to help me, I may accidentally get something I want." Jason Sudeikis

Every day, there is always a new possibility to open connections or potential friends. When I find myself needing help, or needing some advice, who will I go to? The person looking at the ground with an unhappy stare on their face, or the person standing tall with a smile greeting those in passing. I want to be the person people want to feel comfortable around. Being polite and positive does not only help others, but it helps me. When I find myself in crisis and need help, I will know that the people around me will *want* to help because they know I will help them in their times of trouble. To start, I will smile and say Hello, good morning or good afternoon as I enter a room. I want to be the polite light in a dark room. I will be thoughtful, courteous and kind. I will open doors, hold the elevators, and even pick up garbage if it has fallen on the ground. I will not allow someone else's disposition dictate my behavior. I will say thank you and not thanks because thank you just feels good to the soul.

By changing just small features in my daily routine, I can present a completely different outlook to those around me. I am capable of being whatever I want to be and appear however I would like to be represented. If I want to feel great and know that I can count on people, I need to show everyone around me that they can count on me too.

Activity- I will greet each morning like a challenge. When I wake up to when I go to sleep I need to make five people smile. Whether it is just holding, open a door, or thanking the mailman.

Day Twenty

Element of surprise.

"Every time I smile at someone, it is an act of love, it is a gift to that person; it's a beautiful thing."- Mother Teresa

A smile a day can bring anything my way. I love making people smile, and being able to make others smile should be a goal of mine today. It makes me feel incredible to know that someone felt joy because of me, or something I did. I can change the world just by helping someone else change their attitude. When I do this, I also feel the benefit of that warm wonderful feeling on the inside. Today, I will surprise someone. Maybe I will call my old friend that I have not spoken to in a while or maybe I will treat my co-worker to lunch. Giving a little extra every other day or once in awhile can be the uplifting boost to their day, and also mine. I'll never know how just one extra effort of kindness can help that person.

They might have really needed it that day. Maybe I will surprise someone with help I know they can use. Nevertheless, I will surprise someone today, because being the kind of person that helps others makes my heart smile. If you feel a little nervous about confrontation still, no worries, instead try to pay for the coffee behind you in a drive through or drop off an anonymous donation.

Activity: Every morning, whether I just get out of bed or am heading out the door. I will look in the mirror and smile. I will just smile;

nothing else. I will be amazed at how I feel. Every day, I will just smile. I will do it.

Day Twenty-One

Give gratitude.

"It is not happy people who are thankful, it's thankful people who are happy." -Author unknown

I did it! Today I can say I made it through an entire twenty-one-day mind change. It's the 21st day and I do feel a shift in me. Today, I will give thanks and show my gratitude and appreciation throughout the day. I am thankful for the life I have been given. Just because we were born into a situation, does not mean we have to stay in that situation. Whatever life has thrown at me, I am able to come back swinging. I am a better person after this journey and everything I have learned in the last twenty-one days has been a proof of that. Just by me reading this book, I have shown that I want to be the best I can be. Now, I realize that life is what I make of it. I will show my gratitude in a maverick of ways. I will make eye contact and smile at everyone I see. I will leave a thoughtful handwritten note for my loved one to see. I will volunteer my time today. I will pack lunches and hand them out to people I see in need. I will leave a huge tip today. I will tip them before they even take my order and tell them because I know they are going to take care of me. I will pay for someone's food or coffee in front of me. I will thank my creator and my universe.

They say making a habit takes around twenty-one days, and since this journey, I have felt uplifted, grateful, and even forgiving. I am able to do whatever I want and set my mind too. The only person stopping me is me, and I am never stopping again.

About the Author

As a single mother of two beautiful children at the age of 20, she endured trials and tribulations that many only fear of. However, she took control of her life and her mindset and did not let that stop her from becoming successful. She used the positive influences around her, and a new form of thinking to achieve what many thought was impossible for her. All it took was a little bit of believing in herself, now she is a role model for her children and those around her. Outside of being a full-time mother, she became a small business owner and Life Coach. Her goal is to help those who think the world has left them, and changing their form of thinking into knowing that they can help themselves.

"It is my life mission to inspire, empower and encourage greatness within others." – Bridget Myers Gunsby

Follow her on her Facebook page Bridget Inspires to hear her daily forms of motivations and inspiration.

PTP

Pure Thoughts Publishing, LLC